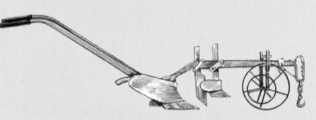

CONTENTS

The
Fireside Book

A picture and a poem
for every mood
chosen by

David Hope

Printed and published by
D.C. THOMSON & CO., LTD.,
185 Fleet Street, LONDON EC4A 2HS.
©D.C. Thomson & Co., Ltd., 1996
ISBN 0-85116-625-3

FRIENDLY SHADOWS

THE light has gone behind the hills
   Where little clouds have danced before,
The darkness waits beneath the trees
   And friendly shadows touch my door.
The bustle of the day has died
   And small, bright stars begin to shine,
I close the curtains on the world;
   Safe and secure, the peace is mine.

The friendly shadows hover near
   With memories of long ago,
And music lifts my heart and soul
   On wings of songs we used to know.
A lamp, a fire, a cosy chair
   Transport me to a magic land,
And I can let the world go by;
   My friendly shadows understand!

Iris Hesselden

RIDING ON THE HILL

THE early day is calling and the lark is soaring
 high;
The breezes in the bracken are a whisper from the
 sky.
Then hearken to our hoofbeats and saddle up your
 horse;
Come, follow where I'm riding, riding through the
 gorse.

For, ever with the sunlight, comes the call again to
 me,
To take the open trail beneath a sky that's wide and
 free.
The silver dews are shining and the woodlands
 re-awake;
Oh! follow where I'm riding, riding through the
 brake.

Oh, I can show you places where the heath is
 scented sweet,
The sky is free above us, and the world is at our
 feet.
We'll race the fleeting shadows, where the winds
 are never still;
Come! follow where I'm riding, riding on the hill.

Iris M. Raikes

BIRCH BOUGHS

BIRCH boughs against the sky
  Delicate and fine,
Etched across the pearl and grey
  In clear, dark line.

The sky so vast would lose
  Some hint of majesty.
If no grey-pencilled branch
  Waved thin and free

Across the distant air.
  The light would paler gleam,
The clouds less luminous,
  Less lovely seem.

With no wind-supple bough
  Of slender light-limbed tree,
Infinity would lose
  Infinity.

Birch bough against the sky,
  How strange that your fragility
Can to the very heavens give
  Awareness of eternity.

Lilian Maude Watts

UNDER THE BLACK FLAG

WE scour the sea, and we care, not we,
    For anything else afloat, we fear
Not galleon, sloop or brigantine.
    We have no dread of the privateer,
Or ships of the King's Navee.

We sight our prey at the close of day,
    And we hoist the dreaded flag.
Then ho! for the long exciting chase,
    For jewel and gem, and bullion bag,
And silks and satins in brave array.

For nothing we fear as the decks we clear,
    All armed for the coming fight.
The guns are trained and the charge rammed home,
    The priming ready, the match alight
For the broadside as we draw near.

Then it's grappling iron and boarding pike,
    And pistol, and cutlass keen;
And hack and thrust, as we cleave our way
    Where the thick of the fighting is seen
Growing ever more fearsome-like.

Then it's hey! for home, o'er the surging foam,
    And the den of the buccaneers,
Where our harbour lies by the coral reef
    Of a Southern isle, where no sail appears
'Neath the sky's blue rounded dome.

Where the wavelets croon in a blue lagoon
    We keep our secret lair,
And drink and feast to our heart's content,
    And our golden hoard of treasure share
In the glow of the burning noon.

C. W. Wade

MIST

ABOVE the trackless moor today
   A curling mist unrolled,
O'er billowy miles of frosted spray
On heather's brown and gold,
And the clear-lined blue of each far height
Slept silent in its fleece of white.

And cold fear crouched ahead
Waiting his chance to spring,
For I moved in a world unreal and dead
Where each familiar thing,
Touched by the wizard mist, would change
To a shadowy shape, confusing, strange.

But the little loch's vague shore,
Where white, pinched ripples lay
In Winter's hand, nor sparkled more,
And the strong sea's far-off play
In dim-seen firs, and a burn in spate,
Galloping muffled, led me straight.

And life is mist-girt now,
And its values, sifted, change;
For the things we prized the most can show
No guidance thro' the strange
New world, while simple things, grown great,
Like courage and love, can lead us straight.

Hylda C. Cole

CAROL SINGERS

DO you remember, do you remember
   Carol singers in the snow?
How we'd rush and peer through the frosted night
As the band struck up with all its might,
Huddled 'neath the lamplight's glow —
Do you remember long ago?

And our youthful hearts with gladness welled
As the singers' joyful anthem swelled,
And the tinselled tree in the ingle-nook
Quaked, as a gust in the chimney shook,
And Christmas bells chimed through the snow —
Do you remember long ago?

And we, untouched by worldly woe
Gazed entranced at the stars and snow,
Listened to that magic band,
Deemed the world a blessed land,
Joyful as the carols sung —
Do you remember when we were young?

Eileen Melrose

NEW YEAR'S EVE

BRIGHT rain is churning
All the shining pools:
The landscape blurs.

The wind comes stirring
All the bracken braes
And bends the firs.

The cold is plucking
The last lingering leaves,
And frosts the dew.

The past is plucking
At the old year's sleeves.
I greet the new!

Malcolm K. MacMillan

JACK FROST

THE door was shut, as doors should be,
  Before you went to bed last night;
Yet Jack Frost has got in, you see,
  And left your window silver white.

He must have waited till you slept,
  And not a single word he spoke,
But pencilled o'er the panes and crept
  Away again before you woke.

And now you cannot see the trees
  Nor fields that stretch beyond the lane;
But there are fairer things than these
  His fingers traced on every pane.

Rocks and castles towering high;
  Hills and dales and streams and fields;
And knights in armour riding by,
  With nodding plumes and shining shields.

And here are little boats, and there
  Big ships with sails spread to the breeze;
And yonder, palm trees waving fair
  On islands set in silver seas.

For, creeping softly underneath
  The door when all the lights are out,
Jack Frost takes every breath you breathe
  And knows the things you think about.

He paints them on the window pane
  In fairy lines with frozen steam;
And when you wake you see again
  The lovely things you saw in dream.

Gabriel Setoun

ODE

WE are the music-makers,
   And we are the dreamers of dreams,
Wandering by lone sea-breakers,
   And sitting by desolate streams;
World-losers and world-forsakers,
   On whom the pale moon gleams;
Yet we are the movers and shakers
   Of the world for ever, it seems.

With wonderful deathless ditties
   We build up the world's great cities,
And out of a fabulous story
   We fashion an empire's glory:
One man with a dream, at pleasure,
   Shall go forth and conquer a crown;
And three with a new song's measure
   Can trample an empire down.

We, in the ages lying
   In the buried past of the earth,
Built Nineveh with our sighing,
   And Babel itself with our mirth;
And o'erthrew them with prophesying
   To the old of the new world's worth;
For each age is a dream that is dying,
   Or one that is coming to birth.

Arthur William Edgar O'Shaughnessy

WINTER NIGHT

MY window-pane is starred with frost,
  The world is bitter cold tonight,
The moon is cruel, and the wind
  Is like a two-edged sword to smite.

God pity all the homeless ones,
  The beggars pacing to and fro,
God pity all the poor tonight
  Who walk the lamp-lit streets of snow.

My room is like a bit of June,
  Warm and close-curtained fold on fold,
But somewhere, like a homeless child,
  My heart is crying in the cold.

Sara Teasdale

ONCE WE SHARED . . .

OH, once we shared together
   Delights you still may know —
Sunlit water, and lofty skies
   Where clouds a-drifting go,
Frosty windows, and wind-screwed eyes,
   Rain on the roof, and snow —
Oh, every sort of weather
   That England has to show.

And once we walked and whispered
   Beneath the English night:
Charles's Wain went a-rumbling round
   Keeping the North in sight,
Rumbling round, not a single sound,
   Laden with silver light.
Oh, once we walked and whispered
   Where you may walk tonight.

Where once we watched the breaking
   Of waves upon the shore,
Tasting salt from the driven spray
   On lips so sweet before,
Watch the sea all the livelong day
   Flinging the stones ashore;
Be glad, for all the aching,
   Though I am there no more.

John Buxton

THE THAW

THE thaw has come to the world at last,
   And slowly melted away the snows;
The trees are stirred from their Winter hush,
   Again the brook down the valley flows.

Bright raindrops hang on the lacing boughs;
   The birch-twigs glow with a purple-red;
While down the moss-grown ride, a jay
   With chattering cry flies overhead.

But, best of all that the thaw can bring
   Is joyful music, the welcome sound
Of hoofbeats echoing down the rides,
   The mellow notes of a questing hound.

A wave of challenging, eager forms,
   That drive through heather and fern and brake;
The chink of bit-bars, the drumming hoofs,
   And clarion horn the land shall wake!

Iris M. Raikes

SPRING IN DORSET

O, WHO am I and what my house,
   And wherefore set so high,
That I should be alive on earth
   Beneath the open sky;

That I should be alive on earth
   In Dorset in the Spring
To watch the bluebells come to birth
   And hear the chaffinch sing?

O, who am I and what my house
   That I should keep such state,
And have such minstrels sing to me
   From early morn to late;

And have such odours thronging me
   And touch each goodly thing—
The gorse, the grass, the willow tree—
   In Dorset in the Spring?

Anna Bunston de Bary

THE LAMBING CHAIR

OAK warm by the hearth, the old lambing chair
    stood,
Side-winged and panelled, high patina wood
From the years handed down from father to son,
A refuge and ease from days' labour — hard won.

The curved lines enfolded him — shut out the storm,
In the crook of his arm, a small, sleeping form
Of a newly-born lamb by the life-giving fire,
As the cattle stirred restlessly — crowding the byre.

The shepherd laid gently the lamb to the floor,
Took family Bible from the shelf by the door,
Mused over dates, ink-blurred and dim,
Treasured milestones of memories, so dear to him.

The lambing chair stands now at ease in a room
Far from bleak hills, stone walls and the loom,
Still cherished and loved it looks out on a quay
To a jigsaw of houses tumbling down to the sea.

Kathryn L. Garrod

THE CALL OF THE KYLES!

I WILL wake from my dreaming,
  And with light step I'll go
Where the sunbeams are gleaming
   On the whins of Glen Croe;
With a view of the Cobbler,
   And the road to Argyll,
Oh! I'll ever remember
   The lure of each mile!

By the paths of my knowing,
   With a song in my heart . . .
It's a gift in the going,
   It's a thrill from the start!
By the quiet of Saint Cath'rines
   And the shores of Loch Fyne,
Oh! the fairest of fortunes
   Will surely be mine!

Down to sweet Tighnabruaich —
   The waters of Kames,
Where the bright gulls make music
   With the beauty of names;
There I'll tramp through the heather,
   While the moon gently smiles
As I joyfully answer
   The call of the Kyles!

Edward Borland Ramsay

FIRST LOVE

IT was here, I remember, I met the girl
   Of my dreams
And I but a boy, with the eye
   Just beginning to see.
It was Spring and the early morn,
   And the sun's warm beams
Were stirring the bird on the branch
   And the bud on the tree.

She walked with her bright brown head
   Held high like a queen,
But her eyes were friendly, the curve
   Of her mouth was kind;
And I, for the very first time
   In the life I've seen,
Fell in love with the girl who has never
   Gone out of my mind.

It is sixty long years and a good bit more
   Since we met
And passed without word or sign: but
   Today I knew
My heart leapt high in my breast — like a
   Youngster's, yet! —
Rememb'ring the sun on her cheek —
   And her eyes of blue.

Sydney Bell

THE SONG OF THE
WANDERING AENGUS

I WENT out to the hazel wood,
   Because a fire was in my head,
And cut and peeled a hazel wand,
      And hooked a berry to a thread;
And when white moths were on the wing,
      And moth-like stars were flickering out,
I dropped the berry in a stream,
      And caught a little silver trout.

When I had laid it on the floor
      I went to blow the fire aflame,
But something rustled on the floor,
      And someone called me by my name;
It had become a glimmering girl
      With apple blossom in her hair
Who called me by my name and ran
      And faded through the brightening air.

Though I am old with wandering
      Through hollow lands and hilly lands
I will find out where she has gone,
      And kiss her lips and take her hands;
And walk among long dappled grass,
      And pluck till time and times are done
The silver apples of the moon,
      The golden apples of the sun.

W. B. Yeats

SPRING CLEANING

AT last we've had a spring-clean,
    The attic now is bare,
And all that's left are odds and ends,
    Some cupboards and a chair.

We feel triumphant, happy,
    That all our junk is moved,
A twenty-five years clear-out,
    Was possible we've proved.

But now the shed is bulging,
    Outside the house a mess,
The overcrowded garage is
    A problem we confess.

Because it's to be sorted,
    The place is like a tip,
We've postponed further moving,
    Until we hire a skip.

It's not the actual clearing,
    But what to throw away,
For things might come in handy,
    So we'll leave them for today.

Chrissy Greenslade

SIX MONTHS OLD

FIND a chestnut candle,
  Very white and straight,
Find a yellow primrose
  Shy and rather late,
Lady's-smock and cowslip,
  Broom of brightest gold,
Find them for Miranda
  Who is six months old.

Half a chestnut candle
  For this day is meet;
Half a pretty lady's-smock
  Might be short and sweet.
But what's the good of snippets
  Or *half* a cake for tea;
When one small Miranda
  Is all the world to me?

Half a year she's travelled
  From fogs and muffin bells,
Now the sunshine wakes her,
  Now the cuckoo tells
Every thrush and chaffinch,
  Every blackbird bold,
"This is young Miranda
  Who is six months old!"

Eiluned Lewis

SPRING LOVESONG

NOW the bright crocus flames, and now
   The slim narcissus takes the rain,
And, straying o'er the mountain's brow,
The daffodils all bud again.
The thousand blossoms wax and wane
On wold, and heath, and fragrant bough,
But fairer than the flowers art thou,
Than any growth of hill or plain.

Ye gardens, cast your leafy crown
That my Love's feet may tread it down,
Like lilies on the lilies set;
My Love, whose lips are softer far
Than drowsy poppy petals are,
And sweeter than the violet!

Andrew Lang

FROM THE OLD VICARAGE, GRANTCHESTER

AH, God! to see the branches stir
        Across the moon at Grantchester!
To smell the thrilling-sweet and rotten
Unforgettable, unforgotten
River-smell, and hear the breeze
Sobbing in the little trees.
Say, do the elm-clumps greatly stand,
Still guardians of that holy land?
The chestnuts shade, in reverend dream,
The yet unacademic stream?
Is dawn a secret shy and cold
Anadyomene, silver-gold?
And sunset still a golden sea
From Haslingfield to Madingley?
And after, ere the night is born,
Do hares come out about the corn?
Oh, is the water sweet and cool,
Gentle and brown, above the pool?
And laughs the immortal river still
Under the mill, under the mill?
Say, is there Beauty yet to find?
And Certainty? and Quiet kind?
Deep meadows yet, for to forget
The lies, and truths, and pain? . . . oh! yet
Stands the Church clock for ten to three?
And is there honey still for tea?

                                    Rupert Brooke

BOYS THEN AND NOW

"MORE than one cuckoo?"
   And the little boy
Seemed to lose something
   Of his Spring joy.

When he'd grown up
   He told his son
He'd used to think
   There was only one,

Who came each year
   With the trees' new trim
On purpose to please
   England and him:

And his son — old already
   In life and its ways —
Said yawning: "How foolish
   Boys were in those days!"

Thomas Hardy

HOME TO MY LOVE

LONG are the hours the sun is above,
But when evening comes I go home to my love.

I'm away the daylight hours and more,
Yet she comes not down to open the door.

She does not meet me upon the stair —
She sits in my chamber and waits for me there.

And she lets me take my wonted place
At her side, and gaze in her dear, dear face.

There as I sit, from her head thrown back
Her hair falls straight in a shadow black.

And in my wearied and toil-dinned ear,
She says all things that I wish to hear.

Dusky and duskier grows the room,
Yet I see her best in the darker gloom.

When the winter eves are early and cold,
The firelight hours are a dream of gold.

And so I sit here night by night,
In rest and enjoyment of love's delight.

But a knock at the door, a step on the stair
Will startle, alas, my love from her chair.

If a stranger comes she will not stay:
At the first alarm she is off and away.

And he wonders, my guest, usurping her throne,
That I sit so much by myself alone.

Robert Bridges

ANEMONES

I WANDERED through a wood of white anemones;
The wind was cold as water from a spring.
It breathed the exaltation of its own austerities,
    And carved in clarity each living thing;
A wind of bright integrity, clear and keen as ice,
The wind that ushered in the fire and the still, small
    voice.
Young wheat flowed water-green across the open
    field,
And veins of green and silver shot through trees
With marble coolness where the sun their Winter
    buds unsealed.
    Through the cherry's white and airy frieze
The light fell, blossom-blanched, as pale and shy,
Wind-fickle, swift to fall and flit, as first white
    butterfly.

Only the glow of primroses and pollened palm
    And kindled spirit are the auguries
Of those swift-coming, sweeping flames that shall
    consume the calm,
    Break through this beauty with new ecstasies,
Spread through the ardent earth until the stars and
    sun
Are challenged by the living fires in this white peace
    begun.

Lilian Maude Watts

IF THOU WERT MINE

IF thou wert mine to love and fold
   Within my arms, and all the gold
And glory of thy gleaming hair
Were mine to clasp and kiss, and there
Close to my heart of hearts to hold:

Then all the joy that e'er was told
Of love in distant days of old
Should light our way, my lady fair,
If thou wert mine!

Dear, though the envious world were cold,
And grief's grey waves about us rolled,
I'd laugh at every little care
And bring to thee, my sweet, to wear
The flower of love made manifold,
If thou wert mine!

Herbert Kennedy

SIMPLE JOYS

BE it not mine to steal the cultured flower
  From any garden of the rich and great,
Nor seek with care, through many a weary hour,
    Some novel form of wonder to create.
Enough for me the leafy woods to rove,
    And gather simple cups of morning dew,
Or, in the fields and meadows that I love,
    Find beauty in their bells of every hue.
Thus round my cottage floats a fragrant air,
    And though the rustic plot be humbly laid,
Yet, like the lilies gladly growing there,
    I have not toiled, but take what God has
      made.
My Lord Ambition passed, and smiled in scorn:
I plucked a rose, and, lo! it had no thorn.

George John Romanes

THE VILLAGE LAD

I'M just a noisy village lad
  And any bit of peace once had
By poor, long-suffering village folk
Is shattered when I laugh and joke
And sing and whistle down the street —
The loudest lad you'd ever meet.
And so they beg me, "Quiet, please!"
They want to hear the hum of bees,
And listen to the lilting thrush
And hear the nearby river rush.
But when the Winter closes round
And silences each Summer sound,
When bird-song fades in frosted tree
And everything's still as can be —
It's then they might be really glad
Of me, their noisy village lad!

Alison Mary Fitt

BRIDLEWAY THROUGH SUMMER

PRECIOUS days of Summer, flying
   On the wings of sunlit hours;
Spring, a memory of beauty,
   Gay, between the showers.

Bridleways and lanes of England,
　　Winding o'er the countryside,
Lure us through the scented hedgerows,
　　Out again, to ride.

On the upland turf our horses
　　Lather as we swiftly pass;
Idle by the brook, to let them
　　Snatch the wayside grass.

With the hush of evening falling
　　O'er the land, its dying light
Down the bridleway we'll follow
　　To the coming night.

Iris M. Raikes

JUNE EVENING

THE evening air of June is sweet,
  With fragrance of the garden musk.
Outlined by twilight I can see
  The nodding roses in the dusk.

The moon and stars are glinting through;
  The birds have settled in their nests.
The rhythm changes, all is hushed.
  And in the stillness, Nature rests.

I feel part of an ordered plan
  As I draw strength from this quiet scene.
June evening of the perfumed flowers,
  You teach me how to be serene.

Joyce Frances Carpenter

ON THE CLIFFS

WHITE foam flying,
　　Grey gulls crying,
Wild waves rolling far across the sobbing sea;
Wet winds wailing,
Cold clouds sailing,
And all the wide world empty, dear, save just for
　　you and me.

Blue wave breaking,
Soft winds waking
A million merry ripples on the smiling Summer sea;
Red cliffs glowing,
Wild rose blowing,
And all the wide world empty, dear, save just for
　　you and me.

White sails gleaming,
Two hearts dreaming,
As love's low whisper wandereth across the silent
      sea —
In rain or sunny weather
So long as we're together,
What matters all the world, my dear, for you're the
      world to me.

Herbert Kennedy

SQUIRREL

At the bottom of my garden
  Stands an old walnut tree.
As I'm digging in the rose-bed,
  Two eyes are watching me.
Each day I put out peanuts
  And little bits of bread.
One day I had my just reward —
  A WALNUT ON MY HEAD!

Now leaves begin to wither,
  Chill mists begin to creep.
My little friend up in the tree
  Quite soon will be asleep.
The winter's here, I'll miss him
  But, I couldn't ask for more
Than a pile of dried-up acorns
  Which he left outside my door.

Olwen M. Neale

THE STONY PATH

I LOVE this stony path of ours
In Summer fringed with fragrant flowers
In Winter covered deep in snow,
I use it when I come and go.

And musing on it memories reach
Back to my childhood on the beach,
Helping my father in the sun
To gather stones up, one by one.

Then watching him, as toiling, bent,
Unwavering from his intent,
He laid them orderly and neat
To make a pathway for our feet.

Now though the years have slipped away
I walk upon it every day,
A symbol of Dad's love and care —
Small wonder that I linger there!

While mincing up some tarmac drive
May be the grand way to arrive,
I know wherever I may roam
Our stony path will lead me home.

Alison Mary Fitt

FRIGATE OF FANCY

ON the lip of the low horizon,
 Free of the sea and sky,
Mistress of wind and current
 Where only the clouds go by,

She hovered a splendid moment,
 Like a sea-bird abreast the gale;
Then dream-pale in the twilight,
 With sunset-crimsoned sail,

She swept on tides of silence
 Where the seas of the sunset gleam,
Bound with a cargo of treasure
 For shimmering shores of dream.

Malcolm K. MacMillan

SUNSHINE

AWAY with Sorrow! Summer in her pride
   Is here among us: earth and sky and sea,
    The basking mountains, woodland, lawn and lea,
Are radiant as a bridegroom with his bride;
Bees hum soft music, flowers are multiplied,
      The birds call to their young from every tree,
    And all live things, rejoicing but to be,
Make their glad presence known on every side.

Away with Sorrow! Let the foul witch go;
      Too cruel are her spells, too keen the smart
    Of her dark sorceries and soul-shaking charms;
Summer is for the joyful; even so
    Let joy, red-lipped, come leaping to my heart
    As leaps a lost child to her father's arms.

Latimer McInnes

LAVENDER'S FOR LADIES

L AVENDER'S for ladies, an' they grows it in the
garden;
Lavender's for ladies, and it's sweet an' dry an'
blue;
But the swallows leave the steeple an' the skies
begin to harden,
For now's the time o' lavender, an' now's the time o'
rue!

"Lavender, lavender, buy my sweet lavender,"
All down the street an old woman will cry;
    But when she trundles
    The sweet-smellin' bundles,
When she calls lavender — swallows must fly!

Lavender's for ladies (Heaven love their pretty
faces);
Lavender's for ladies, they can sniff it at their ease,
An' they puts it on their counterpins an' on their
pillowcases,
An' dreams about their true-loves an' o' ships that
cross the seas!

"Lavender, lavender, buy my sweet lavender."
Thus the old woman will quaver an' call
    All through the city—
    It's blue an' it's pretty,
But brown's on the beech-tree an' mist over all!

Lavender's for ladies, so they puts it in their presses;
Lavender's for ladies, Joan an' Mary, Jill an' Jane;
So they lays it in their muslins an' their lawny
Sunday dresses,
An' keeps 'em fresh as April till their loves come
'ome again!

"Lavender, lavender, buy my sweet lavender,"
Still the old woman will wheeze and will cry.
    Give 'er a copper
    An' p'raps it will stop 'er,
For when she calls lavender Summer must die!

Patrick R. Chalmers

SUMMER RAIN

SEE, the clouds are parting, shining
  Where the sunlight gleams again;
Mist is rolling up the valleys
  Drenched so long in Summer rain.

While our dripping harvest waiting
  Where the shattered corn-stooks stand,
Warms at last with light, caressing
  Once again a golden land.

But, through rain and storm, or sunlight,
  Swiftly pass the precious days;
Memories that will forever
  Linger down the bridleways.

Every trail we ride together
  Holds a charm that cannot die;
By the hills, or through the coverts,
  Where the faltering shadows lie.

I am calling you to travel
  Down the ways we love and know,
While the Summer's fading glory
  Merges into sunset's glow.

As the shadows fall behind us,
  Bright the road shines far ahead,
To the clear horizon, dawning
  Of our dreams, when night has fled.

                                        Iris M. Raikes

THE BLUE QUILT

HERE'S a little blue quilt to cover you, dear —
It's blue like the sky when the weather is clear,
Its silvery sheen is close set with the bloom
Of pink apple blossom to perfume your room,
For I think that the prettiest possible thing
Is a spray of pink blossom on blue skies of Spring.

So although it is Autumn, and Winter is near,
And the wind round our nursery howls lonesome
    and drear,
We'll rock in our chair by the fire, and we'll sing
Till you fall asleep, and you dream it is Spring,
For here sewn together, oh, delightful surprise,
Are birdsong and blossom and sunshiny skies!

Mabel V. Irvine

DIVINE ORDER

GRAZE, gentle sheep,
  And float serenely, swan;
Ebb tides and flow,
Swift rivers, journey on;
Spread, forest trees,
Bring forth new leaves to birth;
Fall softly, snow,
Be still, all troubled earth.

Grow, springing corn,
And fly, migrating bird;
Rise, sun at dawn;
Wind, let your voice be heard.
Shine, stars at night,
Sail, moon, your cloudy sea;
Man, keep your word
As God would have it be.

Marion Holden

THE WINDING ROAD

COME, let us go a walk today
  Along a road not far away
That winds and wends beyond the wood,
The exercise will do us good!

When you and I were in our prime
We simply never had the time
To dilly-dally, young and strong
And full of dreams, we dashed along.

But there's no need to beat the clock
These days, we just enjoy our walk
And look around at this and that,
As side by side, we stroll and chat.

Sometimes we have naught to say
But step in silent harmony
Slowly, as we're not so supple
Being an oldish kind of couple!

The road of life is just like this,
And I can't think of greater bliss
As it winds onwards year by year,
Than being on it with you, my dear.

Alison Mary Fitt

THE CRABBÈD PLUM

AND thou, o small sad savage plum,
   Biting with bitter sting,
Hast thou forgotten Summer's sun?
   The shining pomps of Spring?

Hast thou forgotten how that Spring
   Mantled thy lovely head
In hoodings of rose topaz bloom,
   Bright as the dawn's bright tread?

Hast thou forgotten how that sun
   Nurtured thy tender roots,
Thy Grecian leaves of honey bronze,
   Thy young green eager fruits?

And now thy winding-sheet of gold —
   Thy hundred amber plums —
All the whole bright, wild pageantry
   That rich September sums . . .

Should not this past so beautiful
   Thy present ills assuage?
Should not the sweetness of thy youth
   Mellow thy crabbèd age?

Nina Cust

DEPARTED DOVE

WHEN I was young and deep in love
With darling Daisy May,
My fond heart held a dainty dove
That nestled there each day.

The gentle seasons soon were spent
In pleasant paradise;
But wistful winds of Autumn meant
A muted sacrifice.

And so, in solitude apart
I thought on love alone;
But when I looked within my heart
My dainty dove had flown.

Edward Borland Ramsay

ALONG THE ROAD

HEAR the music of trotting hoofs
   And roll of wheels on the road again;
Know the joy of the open way,
   With jingle of bit and chain.

Look ahead, between two cocked ears
   Rakish forelock is flying free;
Ours the range of the country, when
   You travel the road with me.

See the sweep of the lovely land,
   Winds that ripple the waving grass;
Catch the scent of the meadowsweet
   Along the lanes we pass.

Trot along, little mare, you share
   With us many a golden day;
While the beat of your hoofs rings out
   To charm our cares away.

Iris M. Raikes

HIGHLAND CROFT

I LOVE the coast of Africa where trade winds roar
And the jewelled sea breaks on a sun-drenched shore,
And the day's a blaze of blossom and rainbowed birds in flight,
And the palms sing softly in the scented night.

I love the slopes of Switzerland with snow peaks glowing,
Winding paths meandering, alpines blowing,
Chalets bathed in blossom to the hillside clinging
And down in misty valleys the cow-bells ringing.

I love the villages of France steeped in ancient lore,
Crooked streets a-twisting and the old man at his door,
Cafe umbrellas a-flutter in the breeze,
And out in the fields yellow, sunflower seas.

But deep in my heart one place is calling
And I see a moor with twilight falling,
And the only sounds are the brown burns flowing
O'er the silent land, and the heather blowing.

And the peat smoke drifts at the close of day,
While salty winds in the grasses play
Where a croft house waits with a weathered door
By a path that winds to a lonely shore.

Eileen Melrose

WEATHERS

THIS is the weather the cuckoo likes,
   And so do I;
When showers betumble the chestnut spikes,
And nestlings fly;
And the little brown nightingale bills his best,
And they sit outside the "Traveller's Rest,"
And maids come forth sprig-muslin drest,
And citizens dream of the South and West,
And so do I.

This is the weather the shepherd shuns,
And so do I:
When beeches drip in browns and duns,
And thresh, and ply;
And hill-hid tides throb, throe on throe,
And meadow rivulets overflow,
And drops on gate-bars hang in a row,
And rooks in families homeward go,
And so do I.

Thomas Hardy

CONTENTMENT

CONTENTMENT, said the little lad, his freckled
    face aglow,
Is going fishing with my dad — we're such good
    pals, you know!
Upon the riverbank we stand, in hope, the livelong
    day,
And how Mum laughs when we describe the ones
    that got away!

Contentment, said the bright-eyed girl, is loving my
    boy so,
That he is with me, in my heart, wherever I may go,
It's knowing that, though miles apart, wherever I
    may be,
I'm always just as close to him as he is close to me.

Contentment, said the busy wife, with children,
    one, two, three,
Is giving them the loving care my mother gave to
    me,
And knowing that, in years to come, however far
    they stray,
They'll know there is a home for them if they come
    back some day.

Contentment said Great-grandfather, is sitting in
    the sun,
When all the runner-beans are in, and all the
    weeding's done,
A bit of baccy in my pipe, my dog's head at my
    knee,
And sparrows chirping, fit to burst, in my old
    cherry-tree!

Kathleen O'Farrell

Phillips.

BEAUTY

THE heart of youth is like a flower
  That loves to greet the day,
And all the beauty of its hour
  Time cannot take away.

For with the thought of lovely things
  We never shall grow old:
The joy of early morning clings
  To evening's cup of gold.

And we who shed the bloom of years
  Have wisdom in our eyes,
We know that in this heart of ours
  Immortal beauty lies.

Edward Borland Ramsay

THE SONG FOR ME

A LITTLE song, a short song,
   Is the song for me to sing —
Of little hopes, and little loves,
   And gay thoughts on the wing.

A high song, a glad song,
   Of beauties for the eye —
Of shadowy trees and limpid lakes,
   And Summer in the sky.

A sweet song, a warm song,
   Of good cheer for the hand —
Of blazing fires and frosty winds,
   And Winter on the land.

A soft song, a low song,
   Of comfort for the ear —
Of baby smiles and cooing cries,
   The song that's good to hear.

But for my songs I've little words,
   And still less have I grace —
Only the heart to feel and know
   The world a gladsome place.

Mabel V. Irvine

RUNNING ON

SOUNDS of memory are running
  Through the fading day;
Fugitive the moments flying,
  Follow though we may.
I can hear their challenge ringing
Down the years, their music flinging
  On life's chequered way.

We have loved the dawn and sunset,
  Hills and winding ways;
We have roamed by moor and woodland
  Through the fleeting days,
Sunlight, showers, joy or sorrow,
Everlasting hope; tomorrow
  Comes, yet never stays.

Sands of time are drifting onward;
  Who can bid them stay?
Old familiar places growing
  Faint and far-away.
Could we bid life halt, and capture
Once again the joyous rapture
  Of a vanished day!

Iris M. Raikes

BEDTIME

I CLOSE my book, and climb the stairs . . .
    An old man set to say his prayers;
And ere I lay my dreamy head
Upon the snow-white pillowed bed,
I sip my tea, and nibble toast;
And leave some for the friendly ghost
That promises to watch and keep
Myself when I am fast asleep —
Until the morning wakes the skies
To share the goodness God supplies.

Edward Borland Ramsay

COME, WALK . . .

COME, walk with me through the stars, love,
   Travel with me through the night.
We will abandon the world, love,
   Letting it fade from sight.

Come, fly with me on the west wind,
   Over the mountains and streams,
Touching the clouds with our fingers,
   Sharing the unbroken dreams;

Wander through midsummer meadows,
   Lie where the blossom is sweet,
Rain clouds will pass in a moment,
   Rainbows will fall round our feet.

Come, walk with me through the stars, love,
   We'll find a pathway for two,
Walking together for ever —
   I'll sing my love song for you.

Iris Hesselden

The artists are:—

Charles Bannerman; The Thaw, From The Old Vicarage, Grantchester, Boys Then And Now, The Stony Path.

Sheila Carmichael; New Year's Eve, The Crabbèd Plum.

John Dugan; Under The Black Flag, Ode, The Call Of The Kyles!, The Village Lad, Frigate Of Fancy, Highland Croft, Running On, Bedtime.

Allan Haldane; Mist, June Evening, Lavender's For Ladies.

Eunice Harvey; Carol Singers, The Winding Road.

Harry McGregor; Friendly Shadows, Simple Joys, On The Cliffs, Sunshine.

John Mackay; Spring Lovesong, Home To My Love.

Norma Maclean; Jack Frost, Six Months Old, If Thou Wert Mine, The Blue Quilt, Along The Road, Contentment, The Song For Me.

Sandy Milligan; Anemones, Bridleway Through Summer, Summer Rain, Divine Order, Weathers.

Douglas Phillips; Riding On The Hill, Once We Shared . . . , Spring In Dorset, The Song Of The Wandering Aengus, Beauty.

Tricia Rorie; The Lambing Chair.

William Young; Birch Boughs.

Staff Artists; Winter Night, First Love, Spring Cleaning, Squirrel, Departed Dove, Come Walk . . .